TRADE LIKE
A PIRATE

67 GOLDEN NUGGETS TO
SIMPLIFY YOUR TRADING

W9-ART-443

DEBRA A. HAGUE

TABLE OF CONTENTS

ABOUT THE AUTHOR

Debbie Hague began her trading career in 2000 while operating three golf courses with her husband, Jim. In 2005, she left the golf business to trade the futures market full time. After learning many lessons the hard way, Hague now shares her experiences with students as a part time instructor at Online Trading Academy. She remains an officer of the corporation and part owner of the golf courses.

Hague holds a bachelor's degree in business administration from Indiana University. She has six daughters (ages twenty-five to thirty-nine) and sixteen grandchildren. She lives with her husband in Trafalgar, Indiana.

ABOUT THE TITLE

When I was learning how to trade, I spent many hours on a chat room with other traders. Jeff, one of my mentors, would ask if I was still in the trade that we all had taken together. My answer was usually, "No, I already grabbed the gold and jumped ship." Because I had the bad habit of bailing out of trades early, I earned the nickname *The Pirate*. It wasn't a positive attribute when I was grabbing such a small amount of gold. Now I have become another kind of pirate. I've put some pirate-related fun facts throughout the book so you can see why you want to *Trade Like a Pirate*.

ABOUT ONLINE TRADING ACADEMY

Online Trading Academy is a global institution that provides trading and investing education. For the past 15 years, Online Trading Academy has educated over 30,000 students on stocks, options, forex, futures, and long-term investing strategies in its 35 financial education centers worldwide. Online Trading Academy has business relationships with the NASDAQ, CME, and NYSE and has received numerous awards for the quality and depth of its education. For more information visit: www.tradingacademy.com/debbie.

ABOUT SIMPLIFY MY TRADING

Simplify My Trading develops time-saving tools for individual traders. Check out Simplify My Morning, our newest TradeStation indicator that will automatically draw the most crucial levels for intraday traders. Learn more about Simplify My Morning at www.simplifymytrading.com.

ACKNOWLEDGMENTS

Numerous people have helped me throughout my career as a trader. In my immediate family, many thanks to my husband, Jim, who supported me emotionally and financially while I was learning how to trade, and to my beautiful daughters Tameka, Jami, Mandi, Marri, Michele and Victoria, who are amazing and who inspire me to always rise higher. I love all of you to infinity. I would also like to thank my sister Lisa and my mom, Carol, for always believing in me. I am blessed to have you in my life. My thanks also go to my other moms, Betty and Della, for their faith in me, to my dad, Butch Sr., for teaching me to always see the funny side of life, and to my brother Butch Jr. for his awesome sense of humor.

In my professional family, I would like to thank my mentor and friend Joe Hickman for his incredible patience during the hours and hours he spent teaching me how to trade. You are the best and I am forever grateful. My thanks also go to my other mentor Jeff Manson for the many lessons and encouragement; to my partners Renard Damon and Carey McLean for their support in helping this book become a reality; to Dave Brogden, my awesome illustrator, who always shared my vision for the characters; and to my amazing family at Online Trading Academy for your love and support and for allowing me the privilege of sharing my knowledge with our students.

INTRODUCTION

This book is written for people who are learning to trade, but it is not a manual on strategies. Teaching you the strategies I use to buy and sell financial instruments would only be effective in a live trading environment. What I offer here instead is a series of lessons from professional traders and those who are already on the road to mastering the art of trading. What I share with you are lessons from real-life experience, those things that we don't usually find in a book. I have taught well over one thousand students, so this book contains a wealth of experiences. Of course I have plenty of my own too; I learned everything the hard way. When I started, I knew a lot about the market, but I couldn't trade. As my Dad used to say, I had a big hat but no cattle. I made mistakes at first. I blew up my account twice, for example, and came close to blowing it up a third time before learning how to trade successfully. When I first started teaching at Online Trading Academy, I did not intend to share any of these stories. I thought no one else would ever be stupid enough to do the things that I did. As the students shared their own miseries with me, I quickly realized that we all seem to fall into the same traps. After I began to share my experiences with the class, I saw so many heads nodding, and I knew the students had experienced the same things. Some students gave the look that said, "Oh, I would never do that." I knew then that they hadn't traded yet. There are usually only two categories: those who have made the mistakes, and those who will. I don't think this book will prevent you from falling into all of the common traps, but it will save you some time and money by helping you to identify them sooner.

> *"It's fine to celebrate success, but it is more important to heed the lessons of failure."*
> *~ Bill Gates*

"I will tell you how to become rich. Close the doors.
Be fearful when others are greedy.
Be greedy when others are fearful."
~ Warren Buffet

"If you ain't just a little scared when you enter a casino, you are either very rich or you haven't studied the games enough."
~ VP Pappy

1

UNDERSTAND THE GAME BEFORE YOU PLAY IT

Many people begin trading in the markets without understanding the "game." Most aren't aware how much of what they hear and believe is completely backwards. They listen to the financial news at every opportunity, believing their vast knowledge will prepare them for profitable trading. This couldn't be further from the truth.

News reports will tell you what has performed well in the past, and yes, sometimes past performance is an indication of future performance. We lived quite well on the "greater fool" theory for many years. We were taught to buy a good stock in a good sector and hold it. When these conditions are true, the stock is usually at a high. The theory is that we buy high and there's a greater fool behind us that will buy higher. This works great—until it doesn't.

Many investors and traders sat in shock and horror as they watched their portfolios disintegrate in 2008 while their brokers kept telling them that their investments would go back up. Unfortunately, many people remained diligent far too long and then bailed out right before the recovery began.

They just hadn't studied the game enough.

> *"In a bet there is a fool and a thief."*
> ~*Proverb*

KNOW YOUR OPPONENT

Many traders ask this question: "Can they see my stop? It just seems like they go and grab my stop loss."

The reality is that they don't need to *see* your stop loss. I'm pretty sure Goldman Sachs has read your trading books and they know where you would put it. When buying a stock at or near a low, you would probably put the stop loss below that low.

Think about this: if you were a large institution (such as a bank or a mutual fund manager), and you wanted to put on a large position, you would want to buy low. To buy low, you need sellers who are willing to sell low. When a retail trader buys a stock and it drops down to their stop loss, they just became a *seller who is willing to sell low*. Guess who is buying? When lows are broken, other novice traders will sell short on the breakout. Again, guess who is buying?

It's not the fool.

PIRATE FUN FACT: "The existence of the sea means the existence of pirates" ~ Malayan Proverb.

"The degree of one's emotions varies inversely with one's knowledge of the facts."
~ Bertrand Russell

3

TRADE WHAT YOU KNOW, NOT WHAT YOU FEEL

If an institution wants to unload a large long position, two things are certain: the stock is at a top and the seller needs buyers. But how do they get people to buy?

What do most people think when they hear good news, good earnings, or a favorable upgrade? They don't want to miss the big move. Think about any news event. Isn't it always *in the past*? And didn't those good earnings take place *in the past*? A favorable upgrade tells us that a stock has performed well *in the past*. What would that look like on a chart? Would it look like a falling knife? What would we be hearing on the news? Would it have bad news or bad earnings? Would Jim Cramer be hitting the SELL, SELL, SELL button? Of course not.

This stock will probably look like it's going to the moon, the earnings will be fantastic, someone will probably have upgraded it, and CNBC will be interviewing the CEO, who will tell you how well it has performed. If the chart looks like it's going to the moon, this is probably all true.

With all of that good news, more than likely the stock will be at a high. Who sells high? Institutions. Novice traders will gladly step in and help those professionals unload their large positions, only to be left scratching their head wondering why a stock that looked so good would fall right after they bought it.

Now you know why. They played your *emotions* like a fiddle because you didn't have the *facts*.

Vesper Lynd:
It doesn't bother you?
Killing all those people?
James Bond:
Well I wouldn't be very
good at my job if it did.
~Casino Royale

DO YOUR JOB, TAKE THE MONEY

I am often asked if it bothers me to take other people's money. My answer is always the same: No. I am not at their house holding their hand on the mouse and forcing them to take the other side of my trade. And if I were at their house, I would say, "Don't do that, it's stupid."

There's no doubt that trading is a zero-sum game. Someone wins, someone loses. I can't prevent others from donating their hard-earned funds to the market; they must learn how the markets really work. The only thing I can do is understand where the large institutional buying and selling is happening and then do my job and profit from that knowledge.

If I felt guilty and refused to trade, those individuals would still be donating to the market, and *I wouldn't be very good at my job.*

PIRATE FUN FACT: [toasting to their new partnership] Jack Sparrow: "Take what ye can!" Mr. Gibbs: "Give nothin' back!" ~ Pirates of the Caribbean

"Don't tell fish stories where the people know you; but particularly, don't tell them where they know the fish."
~Mark Twain

5

FOLLOW THE SHARKS

Be the remora...

Craig, the owner of the Online Trading Academy in Seattle, tells this story: "In trading, you have to be the remora. The remora fish has a flat, oval suction cup on top of its head which it uses to attach itself under sharks. It's small enough that the shark doesn't care that it's there. Because it's too small to go out and kill the tuna, it lets the shark do the work and then survives on the leftovers. The remora stays safely tucked under the shark watching for his next move."

There are sharks (large institutions) in the market. You have to accept that more than likely, you are not one of them. You probably don't have an account size that would make the shark notice you. The only way for the small players to survive in this game is to watch where the institutions are buying and selling and then *be the remora*.

PIRATE FUN FACT: "Shark bait" - (1) Your foes, who are about to feed the fish. (2) A worthless or lazy sailor; a lubber who is no use aboard ship.[4]

"*If you don't know where
you are going, any road will
get you there.*"
~ Lewis Carroll

HAVE A DETAILED PLAN

If you bought a coffee shop, you would have to decide on many things, including how much you would spend on the beans, what kind of drinks you would make, and how much you planned to charge for them. All businesses require carefully thought-out plans. The owner also needs to have a well-defined list of products, with very specific recipes for those drinks. Customers expect consistency and wouldn't be happy if their Café-Mocha-Vodka-Valium Latte didn't taste the same every time they ordered it.

Trading is a business. You must specify how much you plan to risk in a trade, in a day or in a month (buying the beans). People who don't control their expenses will be out of business.

In trading, we have very specific strategies (recipes) that we use to produce consistent results over time. We know all the ingredients that go into our trade to make it a higher probability. We have to combine those things consistently in order to make a *latte* (money).

PIRATE FUN FACT: Generally, each pirate crew had its own code or articles, which provided rules for discipline, division of stolen goods, and compensation for injured pirates.

"The problem with any unwritten law is that you don't know where to go to erase it."
~ Glaser and Way

7

PUT YOUR PLAN IN WRITING

"How many of you have a written trading plan?"

I ask this question on the first day of every class I teach. About 3 percent of the students raise their hands (and those are almost always the students retaking the class). Do you think it's a coincidence that there is a 97 percent failure rate in trading? Most novice traders don't have a plan or believe that the plan in their head is complete. It is only after they donate to the market that they will be a little more willing to listen to the experiences of professional traders.

After trading for nine months, Kathy came to me and asked me to review her trades. My requirement for reviewing trades is that I must see a written trading plan first. Years of experience have taught me that those without a plan have an extremely high probability of failing. Since I have taught more than one thousand students, this is my way of focusing my time on those whom I can help.

Wanting my assistance, Kathy immediately began to write her plan. She contacted me a few weeks later. "I honestly believed I understood my strategy, but when I went to write it down I realized it had several holes in it." She was completely baffled that she didn't know her own rules, which left her making random and inconsistent decisions while she was in a trade.

I helped Kathy formulate her plan and she is now a consistently profitable trader...but there were a few bumps along the way.

Read on...

"You are the only problem you will ever have and you are the only solution."
~ Bob Proctor

ANALYZE YOUR TRADES

At some point, no one will be able to help you. Scary, isn't it?

I met Kathy at a fantastic little Italian restaurant to discuss her trading. After sharing her frustrations for about twenty minutes, she stopped herself. "You can't help me, can you?"

Unfortunately, she was right. I could not help her without knowing what she was doing wrong. Although I had a strong desire to help, I had no way of knowing if she was swimming upstream by constantly counter-trend trading, placing her stops too tight and doing the slow bleed, buying and selling in the right places or if she just bailed out too early and sacrificed the trades that were trying to pay her.

Kathy and I discussed the importance of a trading journal. I've never been fond of calling it a journal, because what Kathy really needed was a thorough analysis of where she was making and losing money in the market. If she had tracked those few things, she would have known exactly where she needed to make changes, and I would have probably missed out on a delicious dinner.

Once Kathy started analyzing her trades, *she became her own solution.*

PIRATE FUN FACT: "Cat o'nine tails" - A whip with many lashes, used for flogging. "A taste of the cat" might refer to a full flogging, or just a single blow to 'smarten up' a recalcitrant hand.[4]

"Don't look where you fall, but where you slipped."
~ African Proverb

LEARN FROM YOUR MISTAKES

While I was learning to trade, my husband would ask me the same question each night: "Did you have a good day?" My focus was on the outcome of my trades, so my answer was always based on whether or not I made money that day (usually not).

After spending a considerable amount of time analyzing my trades, I learned what I was doing wrong. I discovered that I would have made money if I had executed correctly. I was taking the right trades, but I kept making the same mistake over and over.

After realizing this, I changed my answer. When my husband asked if I had a good day, my answer was based on whether or not I followed my rules and executed according to my plan. I never again answered based on money. He eventually figured out that he wasn't going to get the information he wanted and asked for the statements to be copied to his e-mail.

It was easy to see that I fell because I wasn't making money, but life changed when I discovered *where I slipped.*

PIRATE FUN FACT: 'Swab' - To clean something. 'Swabbing the decks' would be a mild penalty for a disobedient pirate.[4]

*"Today you are You,
that is truer than true.
There is no one alive who is
Youer than You."
~ Dr. Seuss*

10

FIND YOUR OWN TRADING STYLE

There are probably sixty-seven million ways of trading. You have to find a style that's right for you. How much time do you have (hours) each week to dedicate to trading? Do you have a full-time job that you will need to keep while learning? When can you trade (morning, evening, weekend)? Is your goal wealth building or income generation? Do you enjoy being in front of your computer? Are you easily stressed or easily bored? There are so many factors that need to be considered to design a trade plan to fit each person's individual needs. You cannot trade someone else's plan any more than you can wear someone else's glasses.

Joe came into my class after many years of struggling to try to balance his passion for trading, a very successful career, and his family. As I talked with him, I discovered his available time and resources. He could not quit his job and become a full-time futures trader, which was his ultimate dream. He decided he could spend a couple of hours each night after his kids had gone to bed and more time on the weekends. We designed a plan to work toward Joe's dream over a period of time by replacing his income first through longer-term trading and trading in the currency market, which was more suitable to his schedule. Once he had replaced his income, he would continue to trade the currencies, but also spend his days learning the futures market (his ultimate dream). Joe is taking the steps that he can for where he is right now.

There are so many different ways to trade. The key is to find out what is possible with your own set of limitations, and then do not let what you cannot do interfere with what you can do.

It is truer than true; there is a plan that is right for you.

"And since you know you cannot see yourself, so well as by reflection, I, your glass, will modestly discover to yourself, that of yourself which you yet know not of."
~ William Shakespeare

11

KNOW THE DIFFERENCE BETWEEN PERCEPTION & REALITY

One thing that still amazes me is how our perception in trading is so much different from our reality.

Jeff thoroughly believed that he was an expert on trading IBM stock. After analyzing his trades, he was shocked to discover that he had never actually made money on his IBM stock trades.

Eliezer was convinced that his problem was that he was not choosing the right supply and demand zones. After analyzing his trades, he was shocked to discover that he was quite good at choosing zones, but having a tight stop was the reason for most of his losses.

Bob considered himself a trend trader. After analyzing his trades, he was shocked to discover that he had taken more trades against the current trend than with it.

I was convinced that I just didn't pick the right trades. After analyzing my trades, I was shocked to discover that I actually picked very good trades, but by bailing out of them early, I had cost myself a lot of money.

Accept the fact that you cannot see yourself so well and let your journal discover that which you do not know.

"*A child of five would understand this. Send someone to fetch a child of five.*"
~ *Groucho Marx*

12

KEEP IT SIMPLE

Trading is simple; it's just not easy. Why? Because we complicate it. Understanding the imbalance of supply and demand, then buying where demand exceeds supply is a very simple concept that any intelligent adult can learn.

Michelle was working a full-time job while learning how to trade the markets. She had a few hours in the morning to set up her trades, but sometimes they wouldn't play out before she had to leave. Her teenage daughter was given very clear instructions about what to do. Knowing so little about trading, her daughter didn't form any opinions, she just executed exactly as her mom had instructed.

Over time, Michelle realized she was making more money when she wasn't home. When she was home to take trades herself, she had a tendency to form opinions about what might happen and then change her original plan. Anyone who has traded has experienced this. We take what is simple, add all of our thoughts and perceptions to it, and make it very complicated.

It makes you wonder why we don't just go *fetch a child* to do our trading.

PIRATE FUN FACT: "lad, lass, lassie" - a younger person.[5]

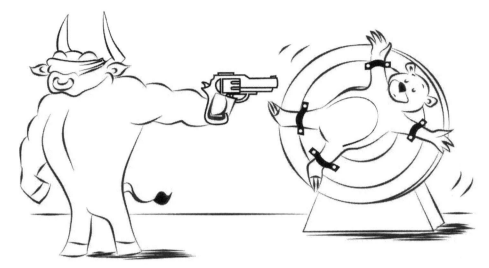

"Next in importance to having a good aim is to recognize when to pull the trigger."
~ David Letterman

13

IMPROVE YOUR ODDS BY ONLY TAKING THE BEST TRADES

I was the classic over-trader. I traded every single day, even when the market was completely random. If it moved, I took a shot at a trade. On one particular day, I took forty trades on the Dow Jones Futures market. Now, for those of you who don't trade futures, let me just say there aren't forty good trades in a day. Actually, if you're trading only the Dow, there probably aren't more than three. I don't know what the other thirty-seven were, but I took them. I looked like Annie Oakley, both guns blazing. The only difference was that Annie could hit her mark.

Over-trading is one of the fastest ways to blow up your account. Not all trades are created equal. We have to learn to find those places on the chart where the best opportunity exists. We also have to recognize when we do not want to risk our capital. You can risk one hundred dollars in the market in a trade that has a high probability of success, or you can risk that same one hundred by gambling in the market.

We have *to recognize when to pull the trigger.*

PIRATE FUN FACT: Pirates preferred to steal the round top treasure chests because they were more expensive and probably contained more valuable contents. Wealthy people bought them to travel on ships because when luggage was stacked, the round chests would be on top and would stay dry.

"Depend on the rabbit's foot if you will, but remember it didn't work for the rabbit."
~R.E. Shay

14

TRADING IS NOT ABOUT GETTING LUCKY

I started playing around in the stock market in 2000. Our family business is seasonal, so I could trade only during the winter months. During this time, the market usually went up, so I actually made a little bit of money. After five years, I decided that I could make a lot more money if I committed to full-time intraday futures trading. It was only then that I discovered the difference between being lucky and engaging in consistently profitable trading. I didn't have the knowledge of institutional buying and selling, nor did I understand the game.

Anyone can put on a winning trade because that's purely luck. Becoming consistently profitable requires skill and discipline, which I didn't have. Once I found myself in a market that was all over the place intraday, *luck didn't work for me any more than it did for the rabbit.*

PIRATE FUN FACT: "Black Spot" - A black smudge on a piece of paper used by pirates as a threat. A black spot is often accompanied by a written message specifying the threat. Most often a black spot represents a death threat.[2]

"The New England Journal of Medicine reports that 9 out of 10 doctors agree that 1 out of 10 doctors is an idiot."
~ Jay Leno

"42.7 percent of all statistics are made up on the spot."
~ Larry the Cable Guy

15

TRADE WITH HIGH PROBABILITIES NOT RANDOM POSSIBILITIES

It is a skill for traders to learn to think in probabilities. Professional traders have learned that each individual trade is only a small part of a bigger picture. As a result, they don't perceive the risks of trading in the same way as the novice. Professional traders have a predefined amount they will risk, and they thoroughly understand that as with all probabilities, they are not 100 percent. We expect the market to take our money at times and we're OK with that. Failed trades are part of the game and not a personal failure.

Because we think in probabilities, it causes us to look at trades differently. We want our edge, so we look for trades that have a higher probability of success. We don't just want to be in the market, we want to be in it only when there is a statistical probability in our favor. Novice traders will enter trades thinking it's *possible* that something might happen.

Professionals trade based on what's *probable*, not what's *possible*.

PIRATE FUN FACT: Barbossa: "It's not possible!" Jack Sparrow: "Not *probable*." ~ Pirates of the Caribbean

*"I always wanted to be
somebody, but now
I realize I should
have been more specific."
~ Lily Tomlin*

16

BE SPECIFIC ABOUT WHAT YOU WILL DO

Many of the trading plans I've reviewed have statements like, "I will buy at the lows," or "I will sell when price reaches my target," or "If the trade is not working out, I will get out". These are not bad rules, but they are just way too vague.

What's a low? How do you know it's a low? Are you going to buy something that's falling like a rock? It's at a low. Where's your target? What criteria did you use to set the target? What makes you think it will get there? How do you know that trade is not working out? If you see one candle that's not in your favor, are you going to close the trade?

Unfortunately, traders with vague rules have a tendency to address these issues differently every time they enter a trade. They don't realize that this creates randomness and random trading is gambling.

We have to clearly define our trading rules before we can follow them, and that means we *have to be more specific.*

PIRATE FUN FACT: "Davy Jones' Locker" - A fictional place at the bottom of the ocean. In short, a term meaning death. Davy Jones was said to sink every ship he ever over took, and thus, the watery grave that awaited all who were sunk by him was given his name. To die at sea is to go to Davy Jones' Locker.[2]

"A short pencil is better than a long memory."
(Old pilot saying)

17

CREATE A ROUTINE

We bought a little Beechcraft Musketeer in 2000. My instructor was very explicit about the importance of the preflight checklist. He wanted to make sure it was clear that no matter how many hours you have flown, you still have to use an actual printed checklist. He explained that many accidents are caused by a failure to check something before leaving the ground. If you get distracted and forget something, like checking the amount of fuel in the tanks, the result can be disastrous. My friend Tucker, who has flown over twenty thousand hours, says this about his preflight checklist, "I'm not depending on my memory, so this thing could save my life".

When I was learning to trade, I found myself getting stopped out of trades because of something I had forgotten to look at that morning. I decided to take the lessons from flying and apply the same rules. I created a checklist for my morning that I follow every day before entering the markets. Some mornings I go through the charts and then glance over the checklist to make sure I've looked at everything. After all these years, I still have days when I've skipped something. What I've discovered is that having a preflight checklist can save my life, and having a pre-trading checklist can save my accounts.

I know *I don't have a long memory, so a short checklist is mandatory*.

PIRATE FUN FACT: "Shipshape" - cleaned up and under control.[5]

"Everyone has a plan - until they get punched in the face." ~ Mike Tyson, Boxer

18

STICK TO YOUR PLAN

Some say that trading is 90 percent psychology. Others argue that it's 95 percent. Unfortunately, most traders focus on the 5 percent to 10 percent academic part and ignore the elephant in the room who is eating their lunch. Having a sound trading plan is not enough. Sticking to your plan even when it goes against you is one of the most difficult parts of trading.

When I first began to teach, I thought I would never share the mistakes that I made in learning to trade. Surely, no one else would be as foolish as I was. After a few classes, I realized that the mistakes I had made were all too common. I heard the frustration in my students' voices as they shared their stories. They knew what they wanted to do, but somehow when they were in a trade, they made a different decision.

Some of you may remember this commercial: "Here's your brain… and here's your brain on drugs. See the difference?" and then they showed a normal brain beside an egg frying in a pan. Just think of that as, "Here's your brain…and here's your brain in a trade. See the difference?"

The reality is that new traders don't usually make good decisions when they are in a trade. Knowing this, traders must make their decisions before entering the market. This comes from having a plan, and following it even when the market *punches you in the face.*

"We cannot change the cards we are dealt, just how we play the hand."
~ Randy Pausch, The Last Lecture

19

FOCUS ON EXECUTING WELL

One of my biggest challenges in class is to get students past the very same mistakes that I made, because those decisions feel right and make sense to us. I know what they are thinking and feeling because I've been there.

Once we are in a trade, we have a tendency to want to change our decisions based on what we are seeing at that moment. It's natural and it makes sense to us at that moment. It looks and feels logical that if the trade is failing, you exit. But what we don't realize is that almost every trade will *look* like it's failing at some point. Very few go straight to the target once we get in. In trying to preserve some of our cash, we end up exiting trades that are trying to pay us. We assume a small risk when we enter the trade but immediately want to pull it back off the table. We do this by moving our stop loss too soon, or by closing the trade with a small profit.

It is a journey in learning before we arrive at a place where we can be happy because we executed well, knowing that this is where our success lies. We cannot *ever* control the outcome of a trade, *just how we play the hand.*

"*A round man cannot be expected to fit in a square hole right away. He must have time to modify his shape.*" ~ Mark Twain

20

MOLD YOURSELF INTO A TRADER

If your shoes don't fit, you don't go buy a new pair of feet. When something doesn't fit us, we usually change that thing that doesn't fit. As much as we try, we can't change the market. We have to change ourselves.

I hate to tell you this, but trading doesn't fit you. It doesn't really fit anyone; traders have to learn to fit themselves into it. How can I make that statement? Because if you are reading this book, there are a few things I know about you. 1. You have an interest in trading (you bought a trading book). 2. You are confident (you believe you can trade or you wouldn't be reading this book). 3. You have had success in your life (where else would you get the funds to trade?). 4. You are a 'thinker' (success comes from figuring out what doesn't work and fixing it). 5. You have an entrepreneurial spirit (you want to take control of your finances through learning about the markets). Successful people usually have a recipe for their success: hard work and attention to detail, and when something doesn't work, they change the process. Unfortunately, this doesn't work in trading.

When you have a well-defined trading strategy, you will execute your trade according to your rules. If that trade fails, you still take the next trade using those same rules. And if the next trade fails, again you execute the same way. Intelligent people have a very difficult time with trying to do the same thing and expecting different results. So as confident, successful, and entrepreneurial thinkers, we try to 'improve the process' when something doesn't work. The problem with constantly tweaking a strategy is that your trading becomes random. Inconsistent trading is not much better than gambling. Just stay in the chair long enough and the market (the house) will take your money.

Trading is difficult because we have to modify ourselves, not the process.

Read on…

*"Remember this:
The house doesn't beat the
player. It just gives him the
opportunity to beat himself."
~ Nicholas Dandalos
'Nick the Greek'*

21

DON'T GAMBLE

Are you the gambler or the house? Is the casino owner gambling? Of course not. The house owners have a statistical probability in their favor and they work that small edge over time. They operate consistently and it pays. Their only job is to keep the patrons in their chairs. If they stay long enough, eventually the gamblers will donate their money. Why? Because the gamblers are random; they don't usually have a plan, and the probabilities are against them.

Trading is like gambling, but you get the choice of whether you want to be the House or the Gambler. If you trade with a well-thought-out plan, with the statistical probabilities in your favor, and you execute consistently over time, you will make money. If you are random, just stay in your chair long enough and the market will take your money.

Realistically, the market can't *take* your money, but *it will give you plenty of opportunity* to donate it.

PIRATE FUN FACT: "Motherload" - The largest amount of booty discovered.[2]

"Never mistake motion for action."
~Ernest Hemingway

22

DON'T OVER-TRADE

I've met many traders who felt compelled to be in the market every day since their job is to trade. You don't have to be in a trade to be working. Many times when you analyze your trades, you will find that a lot of money is lost on days when you shouldn't have even been in the markets.

Professional athletes spend hundreds of hours preparing for an event that sometimes takes minutes to execute. Professional traders spend a lot more time studying the markets and searching for trades than they do in executing trades.

Limit the number of trades you take and don't increase that number until you're profitable. Being in a trade is not what makes you money; it's being in the right trades.

PIRATE FUN FACT: It's safe to assume that life at sea was one great bore for pirates. A great contrast from land life: sailing meant weeks of boredom searching for prey, with only intermittent bursts of excitement as victims were sighted, boarded and then plundered.[1]

"Revenge is often like biting a dog because the dog bit you."
~Austin O'Malley,
Keystones of Thought

23

DON'T REVENGE TRADE

Revenge trading means continuing to trade after a loss because the markets took your money and you have to get it back. This is what causes traders to make all kinds of irrational decisions, such as taking on a larger position, adding to a loser, or over-trading.

After a series of losses one morning, I became determined not to end the day with a loss. I took several more trades that failed, and then I decided that one good trade with ten contracts (instead of one) could recover my day. What I didn't consider was that my judgment was poor that day, and I was getting ready to take that same judgment into the market at ten times the rate of speed. I did this for one reason: I simply hadn't learned to accept my losses.

After a series of losses, shut down your computer. Revenge trading can turn a $300 loss day into a $3,000 loss day. Now how do you think I know that?

PIRATE FUN FACT: "Sea dog" - An experienced seaman[4]

"I've been listening to my gut since I was 14 years old, and frankly speaking, I've come to the conclusion that my guts have sh*t for brains."
~ High Fidelity

24

TRADE WITH SKILLS NOT GUT INSTINCT

There are many people who attempt to trade using their gut instincts. The worst thing that can happen to them is when it works. They are given the impression that trading is easy, they have the 'gift', and they are unstoppable. When this method fails (and it will), they are fully convinced that it's only a small setback and because they have the 'gift', they will get it back. They take large positions on a hunch, believing they'll be back in control soon.

I've heard countless stories about those in 'recovery mode'. Once their losses mount, their confidence is shattered along with their account. It is only then that they accept the truth. You cannot trade with your gut because it has an *odorous waste product from the digestive tract for brains*.

PIRATE FUN FACT: "Poop deck" - The part of the ship farthest to the back, which is usually above the captain's quarters. This is not the bathroom.[5]

*"I do not take a single
newspaper, nor read one
a month, and I feel myself
infinitely the happier for it."
~ Thomas Jefferson
(1743 - 1826)*

25

DO NOT TRADE THE NEWS

I haven't watched local TV news in years because the stations report only negative stories. If no one is bleeding or dying, there's no story. The anchor starts with "Good evening." and everything goes downhill from there. I don't listen to market news either, although I do have it running and muted while I am trading just in case something happens that I should know about.

In order to make money in the market, we buy low and sell high. Think about this: When a stock is at a low, do you ever see market "experts" telling us to buy it? In many instances, they will tell you how poorly it has performed, and more than likely someone just downgraded it. When it's time to take profits on a trade, the stock is more than likely doing quite well, usually with good earnings. The talking heads are going to tell you sixty-seven reasons why they like this stock, and Cramer will be hitting the BUY, BUY, BUY button.

No matter what you are trying to do—buy or sell—the talking heads are going to be there making you second-guess your decision. Are they lying? No, absolutely not. When a stock is ready to sell, it has performed well *in the past*. Trust the charts to tell you how it might perform in the future.

Don't trust the news reports….*and you will be infinitely happier for it.*

"Television news is like a lightning flash. It makes a loud noise, lights up everything around it, leaves everything else in darkness and then is suddenly gone."
~ Hodding Carter

26

WATCH FOR NEWS TO RETRACE ITS STEPS

If you want to see a news lightning flash, just watch as Federal Reserve chairman Ben Bernanke says something negative about the markets or the economy when he presents his economic outlook. The market drops like a rock. It also moves with lightning speed when there's a tsunami in Japan, when high or low unemployment numbers are announced, or when just about anything else happens that seems unexpected.

Have you noticed what happens afterward? The market tends to take back or give back whatever it lost or gained. The amount of time it takes varies from seconds to days or weeks, but the outcome is usually the same. When Big Ben is negative, you could go short for the day, but watch out for the rally the next day. After the tsunami, the market took several weeks to return to its previous uptrend. Some of the economic announcements return so fast that you barely see it happen.

They certainly have an impact on the market, but *like lightning, news generated moves don't last long.*

PIRATE FUN FACT: "Batten down the hatches" - Put everything away on the ship and tie everything down because a storm is brewing.

"I would not waste my life in friction when it could be turned into momentum."
~ *Frances Willard*

27

TRADE WITH THE TREND

I was fortunate enough to observe Sean Kim, one of our instructors, in action. On the first live trading day in his class, Sean gave the students a simple assignment: find a strong stock and go long. Many of the students in the room had no experience at all, and barely knew what "long" meant. He showed them the "buy" button and told them to hit it. The overall market was in a strong uptrend that day. By the end of the day, almost all of the students (except three) were making money. Even though they had lousy entries and didn't know why they were long, they still made money.

Trading with the momentum is like rowing downstream; you really don't have to do much and you'll still go in the right direction. When we trade against the momentum, we are paddling upstream. We must have a very good entry and a very good exit or we lose money. Momentum traders can have a lousy entry and a lousy exit and still make money.

So what about those other three students…

PIRATE FUN FACT: "Haul wind" - To direct a ship into the wind.²

"No problem can withstand the assault of sustained thinking." ~ Voltaire

DON'T OVERTHINK

As I mentioned, there were three students in Sean's class who were losing money.

I asked each of them individually why they were short in the market (the instructions were clear to go long). Remarkably, each of them answered the exact same way: "I *thought* the market would turn here." They were not sitting near one another, so this was not a 'group think' problem. It is, however, a common problem.

As intelligent adults, we like to *think*. Our success in other areas of our lives comes from being able to see a problem, think it through, learn, make adjustments, and move on. This has served us well. That is the normal path to success—except in trading. We must trust our charts and not our thoughts.

One of my favorite comedians, Ron White, sums it up perfectly, *"Next time you have a thought, let it go."*

"What matters is the ability to think different...to think out of the box."
~ Walter Isaacson

29

THINK OUTSIDE THE BOX

Professional traders aren't necessarily smarter than everyone else; they have just learned to think differently. They understand that you have to buy when it looks like you should sell and you have to sell when it looks like you should buy. It won't look or feel logical.

We have to enter into trades without certainty. We cannot study a chart until we know the outcome of the trade, and if we do, it's too late to trade it. We have to accept that anything can happen at any time.

Many smart people have entered into the trading arena only to leave it with a bruised ego and a deflated account. When there is such a high failure rate among very intelligent people, you have to step back and see why. It can't be academic, because intelligent people can learn anything. Retail traders are trained to buy high. "Find a good stock in a good sector with good earnings…" When you find it, that stock is not going to be at a low.

Intelligence alone won't make you a trader; we must train ourselves to think differently.

*"You can discover what
your enemy fears most by
observing the means he uses
to frighten you."
~ Eric Hoffer
(1902 - 1983)*

PIRATE FUN FACT: The Pirate 'Blackbeard' knew that if he looked fright-ening then ships might surrender to him sooner. He let his hair grow and started a beard that would almost cover his face. He twisted his long hair and beard in pigtails and tied colored ribbons on the ends. During battle he lit slow burning hemp cord under his hat near his ears that would smoke and envelop him in a cloud. To add to his menacing appearance he also wore several pistols (as many as six) along with his knives and cutlass at his waist. While in battle the opposing crew often surrendered at the mere sight of him. The fear his new image created had the psychological effect he wanted.

30

KNOW HOW THE SHARKS PREY ON YOUR
FEAR AND GREED

Large institutions know how to trap a novice trader. Most of the mistakes made in trading are very common. This is because logical people try to trade and they try to use logic in the market. This is one of the biggest mistakes that you can make in the market. You cannot use logic or what appears to be right.

Logically, a company's stock should go up after a good earnings report, but it doesn't always do that. Many times, this is a trap. Remember, people are always going to take profits. When large institutions need to sell, they need buyers. And good earnings bring in all the novice buyers.

When we were in a strong bull market, buying high worked over time. Novice traders would buy high hoping there would be someone else who would buy even higher. After 2008, many traders realized this was a mistake. We are no longer in a bull market. If you have been in the market for the last twelve years, you're pretty much back to even. Unfortunately, most people were in late and out late, so they are in a much worse situation.

Observing how the sharks have used fear and greed can enable traders to break free from the trap.

"Life is divided into three terms - that which was, which is, and which will be. Let us learn from the past to profit by the present, and from the present to live better in the future."
~ William Wordsworth

31

STUDY HOW THE MARKET TURNS

Professional traders know what the novices are thinking, because we used to be them. I used to see a market break the previous high and become convinced that we were going to the moon. I couldn't wait to get in, and as soon as I did, I would watch in shock as the market reversed and took my money.

When we break a new high, people who sold short get hit on their buy stops. Breakout traders jump in with more buy orders to go long. As a result, there are plenty of buy orders now to fill the institutional sell orders. Institutions have an average price they need to achieve when buying or selling. If the market falls off a high and they do not get their sell orders filled, you will see the market pushed back up.

If you study the market, you will see some consistent patterns in how it turns. There is almost always a retesting of a level. Sometimes it barely breaks a new high or low, and other times it just retraces its path about three-quarters of the way back. Most traders don't usually like to give back 75 percent of their profits, so once the trade goes in their favor, they move their stop loss to lock in a small profit. When the market retests the level, they leave with a very small profit, even though they were right in the direction. Watching how a market retests a level can help traders fight the fear that their trade is failing and stay in the game long enough to see some real profits.

Learn from the turns in the past and *profit from it in the future.*

PIRATE FUN FACT: "Mutiny" - To rise against authority, especially the captain of a ship.[2]

"Show me da Money!"
~ Jerry McGuire

32

DON'T FOCUS ON THE MONEY

Ask almost anyone why he or she wants to learn how to trade, and the answer will usually be "money." Of course, that's why we are all attracted to trading.

Many problems are a direct result of focusing on money. While in a trade, we move the stop too soon to protect our MONEY. We put on a small stop so we won't risk too much MONEY. We bail out of trades early to make sure we keep some MONEY.

When we focus on execution, we place the stop based *on the chart*. We move that stop only when our rules say we should based *on the chart*. We exit the trade if conditions *on the chart* exist that make sense to do so. A lot of mistakes can be traced back to a focus on money.

Focus *on the chart* and let the market *"show you da money!"*

PIRATE FUN FACT: "Pieces of Eight" - One-ounce, Spanish silver coins worth one Silver Peso, sometimes literally cut into eight pieces, each worth one Real (Real: a Spanish coin and monetary unit that was popular in international trade).[2]

*"Winners plan actions,
they don't plan results."
~ Carey McLean*

33

DON'T FOCUS ON THE OUTCOME OF
INDIVIDUAL TRADES

I saw this funny quote on Facebook: "I've been dieting ALL morning. Am I skinny yet?"

When we decide to get our bodies in shape, our greatest success comes from focusing on doing the workout. We can't expect to have a firm body after that single workout. Even after a week or two, we don't usually see results. It is only after consistently exercising over a period of time that we see results.

Too many times traders focus on a few trades, and get discouraged when they don't see immediate profits. Traders must focus on the statistical probabilities, which means that some trades will pay and some will take your money. We might not see positive results after a few trades.

It is not possible to *plan* good results for any individual trade. We must *plan our actions* of executing all our trades consistently according to our plan and know that *results* will follow.

"People are always looking for the single magic bullet that will totally change everything. There is no single magic bullet."
~ Temple Grandin

34

STOP LOOKING FOR A MAGIC BULLET

I've met many traders who bounce from one strategy to another, one mentor to another, or one technical indicator to another. They honestly believe that there is something out there that will help them earn millions, but they just have to find it. It is very difficult to convince some people that the problem lies within.

They haven't traded anything consistently nor have they analyzed what they are doing right or wrong. Somehow it's easier to believe that the problem is that they just haven't found the right trading software, the right instructor, the right class, the right mentor, or the right book yet. They hang onto the belief that it's out there just waiting for them to find it.

The reality is that most people have either learned to trade the wrong way or they have an issue that they haven't discovered or addressed. Most want-to-be traders run out of money or patience long before they have completed their search for the elusive but enchanting supernatural pellet. It is only after they spend an inordinate amount of time and money that they discover that *there is no magic bullet*.

*"Don't bring a knife to
a gun fight."
~ Unknown*

35

USE CAUTION WHEN TRADING WITH UNDERFUNDED ACCOUNTS

Many individuals make the decision to trade and then set a small amount of funds aside to see if trading is for them. That little account is usually depleted long before they figure out what they don't know.

Initially, you should look at your trading capital from the perspective of how long you have to learn. One of my students had a $5,000 account and was willing to risk $1,000 per day. I explained to him that he had five days to learn. Good luck with that. This isn't exactly true, unless every day is a loser, but looking at it this way helps you to realize that you don't want to get knocked out of the game before you figure it out. Novice traders usually overestimate their understanding and underestimate the other more skilled players in the market.

Entering the market with a small account and little knowledge is like *bringing a knife to a gun fight.*

PIRATE FUN FACT: A piece of eight could be worth anywhere from $246 to $465.

"Barbie gave me unrealistic expectations for my body and the Disney princesses gave me unrealistic expectations for my hair."
~ Unknown

36

SET REALISTIC EXPECTATIONS

Trading is *not* a get-rich-quick scheme. Consistently profitable traders are realistic with their goals. They know that the market doesn't always produce good conditions for trading and it's not an ATM. They are disciplined enough to sit out of the market when the market is not delivering. They understand that anything can happen at any time and there will be losing days.

I've seen beginners who plan to get one hundred points in the futures market every day. They do the math and figure out exactly how long it will take before they land on the Forbes list of the world's richest people. They haven't considered how long it will take them to learn, or how long it will take them to have the risk tolerance to put on those large trades.

Making millions in your first week is about as likely as a girl *being born with a body like Barbie and hair like Snow White.*

"To the man who only has a hammer, everything he encounters begins to look like a nail."
~ Abraham Maslow

37

UNDERSTAND THE DIFFERENT MARKET
CONDITIONS

The market is new every day, but it usually gives off a lot of clues about its mood today. Knowing the market conditions can help us decide how and if we will trade. When the market is trending—moving upward (bull market) or downward (bear market)—we want to be patient and let our winners run (stay in the trade as long as it continues to pay).

When it's range-bound or choppy, we need to take quick profits. *Inside* days (we haven't broken yesterday's high or low, so we are trading inside yesterday's range) are going to take your money if you are inexperienced (and sometimes even if you are!). We must use extreme caution on those days, or not trade at all. Taking quick profits on trending days leaves too much money on the table.

As traders, we must identify the conditions as quickly as possible and then adjust our plans accordingly. When we are early in a strong momentum move, we might use our momentum breakout tool. If we try to use that tool when we break out of a strong supply or demand zone by one tick, we are going to have a lot of losers.

Make sure you have the right tool for the job because *you can't nail everything.*

"In order to properly understand the big picture, everyone should fear becoming mentally clouded and obsessed with one small section of truth."
~ Xun Zi

38

PAY ATTENTION TO THE BIG PICTURE

I remember my mentors always saying, "Look at the bigger picture." But I didn't fully understand what I was supposed to interpret from it. I knew I was looking for direction, but what if it was in an uptrend and that particular day it was down? Then what? Sometimes the direction would help, but many times I found myself just using the smaller charts. I realized later that I was supposed to be looking much deeper than just the direction.

The bigger picture can tell us so much about market conditions, and we know that different market conditions demand different tools or strategies. For example, when you see very small range days with a lot of wicks, you know that this is a time of uncertainty and we should be prepared for a lot of intraday reversals. Larger time-frame traders should be aware that we are possibly nearing a top. If we see larger expanded range candles, trade with the trend and be patient, letting winners run.

We can also look to see if we are early in the curve of a new trend or late in the curve of an existing trend. At the beginning of a new trend, patience pays. If we are late in the curve, counter-trend trades are much safer than they would be early in the curve.

It's hard to see the big picture when you are obsessed with one small section of the screen.

"If you must play, decide upon three things at the start: the rules of the game, the stakes, and the quitting time."
~ Chinese Proverb

39

PLAN THE TRADE AHEAD OF TIME

Never enter into a trade unless you know your entry price, protective stop, profit target, and how you will manage the trade. Your plan should state your specific setup for entry, the placement of the protective stop loss based on the chart, the dollar amount you are willing to risk, how you will decide on a profit target, when you will bring your original protective stop to break even (once the price moves in your favor) and when you will lock in a specific amount of profits.

Intraday traders should have a daily loss limit. Swing and position traders should have a monthly or yearly drawdown. Once our loss limit is hit, trading stops for a period of time. This gives us time to evaluate our trades and consider what new course of action we might take in the future.

Our trade plan contains all of these *rules*. The difference between our entry and stop loss tells us the *stakes* in the game. When we hit our daily loss limit or daily goal, it is *quitting time*.

"You miss 100 percent of the shots you never take." ~ *Wayne Gretzky (hockey legend)*

40

BE DECISIVE, TAKE THE SHOT

In my early days of trading, I would get stopped out by one tick. Then, while I sat licking my wounds, I would watch the trade go on to my profit target. Other times I would sit and stare at the screen thinking, "that looks like a good trade," and then I didn't take it because I just wasn't sure that it would go in my favor.

Many times traders will have the ideal setup and then refuse to take a trade. They are filled with uncertainty about the market because they're not used to losing. They begin to second-guess every decision they make, causing them to miss trades. The problem is that they usually miss the best trades.

In trading, it is imperative that we execute consistently. Do not waffle on the decision when you have a good setup. Act immediately upon seeing your setup, and follow your trading plan exactly once you are in the trade.

Don't let the fear of missing the goal keep you from taking the shot!

PIRATE FUN FACT: Choosing the right ship and the right cargo to pillage, was an essential part of any pirate ship captain's duty, wishing to avoid mutiny. However, failing to attack a promising ship, could also result in a similar outcome, since most of his crew were sailing for a share in the plundered goods.[1]

"If you want a guarantee, buy a toaster."
~ Clint Eastwood

41

DON'T LOOK FOR GUARANTEES

I can't tell you how often a student has asked me, "How did you know that trade would work out?" The answer is that I don't; it is not possible to know. If you wait to see if it works out, you've missed the trade.

Intelligent people don't want to be wrong, so they are uncomfortable getting into trades without knowing the end result. This uncertainty causes hesitation, and that causes them to miss trades. You have to accept that you will *never* know. We must train ourselves to execute according to a well-defined set of rules without thinking about whether or not this trade will work out. Waiting too long for a confirmation after your setup will make you late entering your trade, which increases your risk and decreases your reward.

If the setup meets our criteria, we take the trade, because we know that *trades don't come with a guarantee.*

*"**Trading without a stop
is like jumping out of
an airplane without a
parachute. You'll get away
with it for a little while and
enjoy the ride. But when you
hit the ground, you'll realize
it was a bad idea.**"*
*~ **Unknown***

42

ALWAYS USE A WELL-PLACED STOP LOSS

There's only one reason that traders don't use stops: they don't want to be stopped out.

One of the worst things that can happen is when you don't use a stop and it works in your favor. This gives you the false impression that it was a good idea. You save pennies by not being stopped out on that one trade, only to turn around and lose hundreds on another one. The problems escalate after you take a big loss, because now you're in recovery mode.

I firmly believe that if people would learn to place the stop in the right place, they wouldn't mind being stopped out so much. If you look at a chart, there is always a place where the trade will show that it has failed. If you place your protective stop loss at that location, why would you mind being stopped out? You would be getting out of a trade that wasn't working (and you don't want to be stuck in a failed trade).

On the other hand, why would you place your stop loss at a level where the trade is showing that it hasn't yet failed? That might cause us to be stopped out of a perfectly good trade. Wise traders always use a stop loss and they put it at that place on the chart where they would be willing to exit that trade.

The stop is a *parachute* that prevents a hard hit.

"It doesn't work to leap a twenty-foot chasm in two ten-foot jumps."
~ American proverb

43

SMALL STOPS DO NOT MEAN SMALL RISK

It seems logical at first that a small chart with a small stop equals a small risk. This couldn't be further from the truth.

On a ten-minute chart, you might see one candle at a turn, but if you put that on a one-minute chart, you might see three to five attempts at creating that turn. What we find in small charts is a lot of noise that gives the appearance of a turn in the market. After being stopped out, we see that same appearance again…and again.

Trading with a larger time frame means you don't see all of that noise. You don't keep taking small pokes at the turn and making small donations. When you add up all the small donations from using small charts, you realize the risk isn't low anymore. Putting on a twenty-point stop one time is not the same thing as putting on a ten-point stop two different times. Many times, if the trader had just accepted that larger risk on a larger chart in the first place, he or she would still be in the trade.

Although it feels better to be risking only ten points, what traders are really doing is a slow bleeding. Just remember, slow bleeding still means you're dying, it just takes longer. And both of those *ten- foot jumps are still going to land you in the abyss.*

PIRATE FUN FACT: "Hornswaggle" - to defraud or cheat out of money or belongings

"Take calculated risks. That is quite different from being rash."
~ George S. Patton (1885 - 1945)

CONTROL YOUR RISK

One of the most important elements of trading is learning to control your risk. If you have not learned to control risk, you will be out of the game before you ever get a chance to see if you could become a trader.

The assumption among novice traders is that professional traders get all the trades right, and if they just learn more they can take better trades too. What professional traders have learned to do is control their risk. When they are wrong, they take small losses, and when they are right they let their winners run. It is possible to make money with a less than 50 percent win ratio.

Some of my biggest mistakes early on were failing to get out of the trades that were going against me. I'm not sure why I was so determined to be right. The market is the only one that's right. I would spend an entire day adding on to a short position when the market was going up all day. My thought was that if it had gone up this far, it needed to pull back. As you can imagine, I had huge losses. If I had controlled the risk and accepted the small loss early in the day, I would have been well prepared to trade long that day.

Getting out of the position with a small loss allows you to look at the market with new eyes. And it means you are taking *calculated risks* instead of being *rash* in the trade.

PIRATE FUN FACT: "old salt" - an experienced sailor. "landlubber" - big, slow clumsy person who doesn't know how to sail

"Any time you take a chance, you better be sure the rewards are worth the risk because they can put you away just as fast for a $10 heist as they can from million dollar job."
~ Stanley Kubrick

45

PROFITS ARE MORE IMPORTANT THAN WINS

You aren't getting an A in this class.

Trading is not a 100 percent game. As a child, I was a straight A student. I never took a book home. I can remember playing a game with myself. It wasn't about getting a 100 percent; that was assumed. The game was to turn in my 100 percent paper before anyone else in class. The more time passed in between, the more I won the game. Now before you think I'm bragging, let me just say that somewhere on the road of life there is a balancing mechanism. I forget things just as quickly as I learn them.

When I was learning to trade, my mentor Joe asked me to track how many of my trades were successful out of the last ten. He tried to convince me that a 60 percent win ratio was excellent and more than I needed (which is true). But he was talking to Ms. 100 percent. Where I come from, 60 percent is an F. Completely unacceptable.

So I set out to fix that. I was consumed by my win-loss ratio. What I didn't realize is that you can have a 90 percent win ratio and still lose money. If you risk $1,000 to get $100 and nine out of ten trades go in your favor, you're still losing. (Nine positive trades = $900, one losing trade = -$1,000; end result: -$100).

Before you put your hard-earned capital into the market, make sure you have a trade that could produce at least three times that amount in profit. Now, when I take a chance in the market, *I'm sure the rewards are worth the risk.*

PIRATE FUN FACT: The types of goods pillaged, depended on the type of ship encountered, therefore many pirates were very selective in the ship they attacked, to be certain that the booty received was worth the risks of battle.[1]

*"I have not failed.
I've just found 10,000
ways that won't work."
~ Thomas Edison*

ACCEPT LOSSES AS PART OF TRADING

I like the casino analogies because they seem so appropriate. We've established that the house owners are not gambling; they are working a statistical probability in their favor. Do the owners have to pay out? Of course they do. Who would go to a casino if you could never win? The house accepts losses as a cost of conducting business. If they refuse to pay out, the game is over.

It's the same way in trading. If traders refuse to pay out, they will be out of business. There are several ways that traders try to avoid paying out: by not using a stop, by doubling their position (dollar cost averaging), or by staying in a losing trade. Every time we refuse to pay out, we are making a mistake because all of these lead to large losses. In trading, large losses are unacceptable!

I now understand that losses will occur. The only thing (and the most important thing) I can control is how much of a loss I will allow. I love Thomas Edison's attitude of refusing to see his attempts as failure. In trading, if a trade loses, *we have not failed*. We have just experienced one of the trades that fall into that inevitable loss percentage.

"Being divorced is like being hit by a Mack truck. If you live through it, you start looking very carefully to the right and to the left."
~ Jean Kerr

47

LET WINNERS RUN

Almost every trader has watched a trade go in his or her favor and then turn and take it all back. We all seem to remember that a little too well. After our stop has been hit, there's a natural tendency to look very carefully so we don't let that happen again. We watch for signs and then bail out before history repeats itself. The end result is that we constantly cut our winners short. Those trades that are going in our favor end up paying us very little. When we look at the overall picture, it is impossible to make money this way.

At one point, this problem alone made the difference between success and failure for me. I simply would not stay in a trade. I earned the name *Pirate* because I was known for jumping ship (they didn't know I was only grabbing a few coins). When I went back and analyzed my trades, I noticed that bailing out early had cost me tens of thousands of dollars. The good news was that if I had not left that money on the table, I would have been profitable. I knew that if I would just stay in the trades I took, I would be successful. Once I realized this, I learned how to really *Trade Like a Pirate*!

The market ebbs and flows in getting where it's going, and its difficult to watch. *Look both ways before entering a trade*, but when you're in a good trade, make sure you *grab the gold before jumping ship*.

PIRATE FUN FACT: "Shiver me timbers" - When the wind blows hard on a wooden ship, the timbers literally rattle. This is a cause for surprise and concern...therefore, "Shiver me timbers" is an expression of surprise.[3]

"You can put makeup on a pig, but it doesn't make the bacon taste any better."
~ Scott Turriff

BE OBJECTIVE, EVEN IF YOU ARE IN THE TRADE

It's funny what happens when a person has a position in a stock. They can tell you every reason they should be in it or stay in it, but rarely why or when they should get out.

John had a large position in ABC and asked me to analyze the chart. After a week in class, I was surprised to see that he was violating every rule he learned in this one trade. When I pointed out the obvious (that his chart looked like a nosedive off a tall building with nothing to stop it), he countered with various "yeah buts." I continued to ask John if his recovery scenarios were probabilities or possibilities, but I still wasn't able to reach his rational mind.

Later that day, I found another chart with the same appearance as John's ABC stock and I asked him to walk through an evaluation of it. Using his knowledge of supply and demand imbalance, he was spot-on with his analysis of XYZ. He was adamant that he wouldn't be in this stock, but if he was, he would exit immediately. I pulled up the two charts side by side and asked John what he thought was different about the two. I could see by his reaction that he knew what he should do. Amazingly, John began to list the reasons why his ABC trade was better than XYZ.

You can make up whatever beautiful story you want about a trade, but it's not going to make the loss *taste any better.*

PIRATE FUN FACT: "Hogshead" - (1) A large cask used mainly for the shipment of wines and spirits. (2) A unit of measurement equal to approximately one hundred gallons.[2]

"A journey is like marriage. The certain way to be wrong is to think you control it."
~ John Steinbeck

THE MARKET IS ALWAYS RIGHT

Intelligent people like to control things. They know that whatever is under their control, they have the ability to change it. It is those things that we cannot control (like the weather, natural disasters, or the economy) that we just have to accept.

We have absolutely no control over the market. It is always right; it's going to do what it's going to do. We cannot make it go anywhere or stop it from going where it's heading. The markets are moved by large institutional buying and selling. Our few shares or contracts are not going to change its course.

Accepting this lack of control will allow us to make much better decisions in our trading. We don't try to hang on to losing trades when we know the direction and the outcome is out of our control. What we can do is use the edge we have in trading and keep our losses small when we are wrong.

In the markets, you will lose big if you think you can control it.

PIRATE FUN FACT: "Coxswain" - A person who usually steers the ship.[6]

*"You can't dig with a shovel
and fill with a spoon."
~ Unknown*

50

USE EQUAL RISK AMOUNTS

How many times have you taken an extra large position in a trade because you think this is the "big one". You just know it's going to go. The sun, the moon, and the stars are lined up on this one. Your last few trades have been great, but you haven't made much because of your small share size. But this is it! You put on the big position with complete confidence. I'm guessing that every trader knows the ending. The big trade fails and the little ones run. Why? Because every trade is just another trade.

You can't go into trades "knowing" this is the one. You make money in the market by executing a sound plan consistently over time and letting your edge work in your favor. The truth is, we will never know which trades will go and which ones will fail. What we do know is that some will, and some won't. A trade on which you've risked $5,000 has the same chance of going against you as a trade where you risked only $50.

Keep your trades equal so you will benefit from the winners and take small losses on the losers. It's a probabilities game. *You can't dig a hole with one hundred dollar bills and fill it with pennies.*

PIRATE FUN FACT: "If ye thinks he be ready to sail a beauty, ye better be willin' to sink with her." ~ Pirate Saying[5]

"*My knight in shining armor turned out to be a loser in aluminum foil*" ~ Tiffany Elmquist & Stefani Stevenson (Co-Authors)

51

DON'T ADD TO A LOSING TRADE

Don't marry the loser!

If you go out on a date and it doesn't work out, what does it cost? Usually just the price of dinner. You are probably comfortable taking someone else out the next night. That small amount didn't destroy your budget. But what if you had married the person and the marriage didn't work out? That's going to financially define you for awhile.

Trades should be like dates. You take one out, and if it doesn't work out, no big deal. It's a small loss. Successful trading is based on a series of good trades to make you profitable (consistency), not one good trade that will make you rich. When we keep adding to our losing trades or take a larger position size, we've just married our trade. If that trade doesn't work out, we are going to feel it for awhile.

Date your trades, don't marry them. Don't let losers run! If it didn't go the way you planned, get out! The market is always right. And you'll never know *which trade is the knight and which one is the loser in aluminum foil.*

PIRATE FUN FACT: "Scurvy dog" - the pirate is talking directly to you with mild insult.[5]

"If the horse has been dead 10 years, it's time to dismount."
~ Joyce Meyer

52

IF IT'S NOT PAYING YOU, GET RID OF IT

In 2011, I was blessed with the opportunity to teach in Mumbai, India. The Indian students are incredibly dedicated and often asked my opinions about specific stocks. I noticed at the beginning of class, many students asked about Reliance Industries (a very strong company) and I soon realized that many of them held large positions. I asked them this question: If you had an employee that was fantastic at one time but who had failed to produce any measureable results in over three years, would you keep them? The answer was obvious: of course not.

I pulled up a chart of Reliance and showed them that it was completely sideways for over three years. This once fantastic stock had added absolutely nothing to their bottom line for well over three years. I pulled up several other stocks that they could have owned over that same period, and we measured the moves, comparing how many rupees they could have earned with that same investment. A year after leaving India, Reliance was still trading sideways slightly below that same range.

You can only ride a stock or a horse for so long, but when it's dead, *it's time to dismount.*

"Within every adversity is an equal or greater opportunity."
~ Napoleon Hill

53

LOOK FOR OPPORTUNITY IN THE ADVERSITY

One thing that professional traders understand is that buying opportunities are at lows, not highs. When someone waits to see proof that things have turned, two things happen: the profit potential drops as price moves higher, and the probability of success decreases. The longer they wait, the worse it gets. Unfortunately, buyers have been programmed to look for things that will ensure they will buy high. Novice traders wouldn't consider getting into a trade that looks like it's dropping like a rock.

Some don't buy when we are under certain moving averages or when the news is bad. Consider what happened with Exxon Mobil (XOM) during the summer of 2011. The Silvertip pipeline had ruptured under the Yellowstone River in July, spilling oil into the water, so the news was horrible. Then a drop in demand for global oil was reported in early August. Exxon Mobil's stock price was falling like a rock. Seeing this, would you have been a willing buyer? Most would say no, but trained professionals look for these opportunities. On August 9, XOM hit a low of $67.03 a share. Within the next seven days, prices rallied to $74.75, a $7.72 gain.

The public saw the adversity, the professional trader saw the greater opportunity.

PIRATE FUN FACT: "Pillage" - To raid, rob, and sack a target ashore.[4]

"Seek freedom and become captive of your desires. Seek discipline and find your liberty."
~Frank Herbert, Dune Chronicles

54

STAY DISCIPLINED!

When I look back at my early trades, I see a lot of random decisions. The obvious assumption is that I didn't have a plan, but that was not totally true. I had a trading strategy that I was using for almost all of my trades. I entered the trade and placed my stop loss and my target based on this strategy. The problem was that once I was in the trade, the rules went out the window and the discipline disappeared. That left me trading solely on emotion.

After I analyzed my trading and attached a price tag to this mistake, I became very determined to follow my plan. There is no doubt that *discipline* is one of the most important things in trading. Discipline means being specific in writing your plan and following it completely, no matter what.

Trading for a living offers a tremendous amount of freedom, *but you'll have to seek discipline to find it.*

"*Adopt the pace of nature: her secret is patience.*" ~*Ralph Waldo Emerson*

55

BE PATIENT AND WAIT ON YOUR SETUP

If you spend a lot of money on a watch, chances are good you're not going to throw it in the backseat of your car. Those things that we value we tend to treat a little more cautiously. I paid a high price to learn patience in trading. I am very patient in other areas of my life (I have six daughters, so just imagine the teen years times six). Surprisingly, I was very impatient when I traded; I just wouldn't wait on the right trade. I didn't seek out the higher-probability trades so I wasn't using an edge.

I mentioned earlier that I was a serious over-trader. The larger moves really got my attention. I was missing the big move! Jump in! Unfortunately, I usually ended up catching it when it was over. It seems pretty obvious now that if I could already see that it was a big move, I was already too late to enter it.

Learn to look for your setup and wait until you find it before you risk your capital. *The secret is patience.*

"Some days you're the pigeon, and some days you're the statue."
~ David Brent (The Office)

56

ACCEPT THAT NOT EVERY DAY IS YOUR DAY

And some days you're the bug, and some days you're the windshield. My mentor Joe used to say, "live to trade another day." You should have a loss limit that you never violate. Rules like this protect you from yourself.

Swing or position traders should have a weekly or monthly drawdown limit. Intraday traders should have a daily loss limit. The daily loss limit shouldn't allow any more than three losing trades. Even if all the trades were executed flawlessly, we still need to stop. After a series of losses, our emotions have changed. When we continue to trade, we run the risk of engaging in revenge trading or getting into recovery mode.

We have to accept that maybe today is not our day. Traders who continue to trade will usually turn a $300 loss day into a $3,000 loss day. And yes, I did that. More than once.

"Our lives improve only when we take chances - and the first and most difficult risk we can take is to be honest with ourselves."
~Walter Anderson

57

ASSESS YOUR TRADING STRENGTHS AND WEAKNESSES

I don't think I have ever met that one perfect personality for trading. Some might be organized but a little too anal-retentive. Some are disciplined but too risk-adverse. Some can multitask, but they don't have any follow-through. Some are humble, but they also lack confidence and they second-guess each trade. Some might be brilliant, but they over-analyze every decision and miss the opportunity. Some are comfortable with the risks, but they lack the patience to wait for the right setup.

It's very difficult to accurately assess our trading strengths and weaknesses, especially if we've never traded. Before I started trading, I would have said that I was a patient person. Interestingly enough, that was one of my biggest weaknesses in trading. It is very helpful to do a strength-and-weakness assessment again after you have traded for awhile. This will allow you to consider those characteristics as they apply to your trading rather than as they apply in other areas of your life. Many personality tests are available on the web, and they can be very helpful.

After testing yourself, it's imperative to see how the characteristics you uncover about yourself will interfere in your trading. Being impatient can lead to impulsive trading. Being disorganized can mean that you will miss some things. Being overly analytical can lead to a never-ending search for the perfect trade, which doesn't exist. Being overly conservative can lead to a low risk tolerance. Until we do the work and are *honest with ourselves*, we can't really identify those problem areas. And once we identify them, then the real work begins in changing them.

"Learn from the mistakes of others. You can't live long enough to make them all yourself."
~ Eleanor Roosevelt

58

LEARN FROM THE MISTAKES OF OTHERS

You're going to make some of the same mistakes that most traders make, but it's really expensive if you try to make all of them. After hearing the stories of well over 1,000 students, I can safely say that I have made almost every mistake known in trading (there were a few I didn't make).

Learning by doing in the market is very expensive. I share my stories because I believe that when people hear what I was thinking (and they are thinking the same way) and then they hear the outcome of those thoughts (big losses), they can learn to look at their thoughts differently. And since thoughts will eventually become actions, we want to change them before donating to the market. Listen to professional traders.

We can learn a lot from *the mistakes of others, but your account may not live long enough for you to make them all yourself.*

"The trouble with being in the rat race is that even if you win, you're still a rat."
~ Lily Tomlin

59

WRITE A MOTIVATIONAL MISSION STATEMENT

Trading is not just a business; it's a lifestyle! I can remember a time when I hit rock bottom. I had blown up my account twice and was well on my way to a third time. Knowing I could not continue to drain our savings, I prepared myself to go back to work either in my previous career field or in our family's golf business, or to start over in something new. As I weighed the options, I began to realize that no matter what I chose, it would never compare to the opportunity I had in trading. I didn't want to go back into corporate America, where I was working for six partners, and I especially didn't want to go back to working with my husband and managing sixty employees. But if things didn't change, I was back to counting vacation days, fighting traffic, and having a salary cap. I didn't realize it at the time, but that's when I began to write my mission statement.

Trading offers unlimited earnings potential. This meant I would be solely responsible for my own future and I could write it my own way. I could trade from anywhere in the world (beaches, the islands!). I wouldn't have to consult anyone about how I would spend my time or prepare a speech about why I needed a day off. I wouldn't have to listen to employees calling in saying, "My cat is coughing up a fur ball and I can't come in to work." I wouldn't have to play slip and slide on icy roads while commuting an hour to work. This was it! I did not want to do anything else! This became my mission statement and gave me a renewed enthusiasm for trading. I doubled my efforts. I didn't care that I had been beat up by the market. I knew I wanted this and if it took me until I was 167, I wouldn't stop. *I knew for sure I didn't want to be a rat.*

PIRATE FUN FACT: "Bilge rat" - (1) A rat living in the bilge of a ship. It is considered the lowliest creature by pirates, but many pirates take to eating the animals to survive. (2) An insulting name given by a pirate.[2]

"*A man may fail many times, but he isn't a failure until he begins to blame someone else.*"
~ Knox Manning

TAKE RESPONSIBILITY

I am often asked if I can predict whether or not someone will fail in trading. My answer is, "Yes, but only temporarily." When I see someone who is never wrong or never at fault, I would bet that this person will fail initially. Some people think that they would succeed if only they could find the right teacher/strategy/trading platform/school/etc. Their inability to make money in the market is not their fault.

I met Ned, a brilliant twenty-something young man who bordered on genius. During our initial meeting, Ned explained that he was absolutely convinced that he could learn anything if only he had the right teacher. Knowing his background, I didn't disagree with his assessment of his intelligence. In our brief time together, Ned refused to get out of several trades, even though the market had clearly reversed direction. When I asked him why he refused to take the small loss, he explained that he was using his patience by staying in the trade. We discussed the importance of accepting small losses, but it was apparent to me that Ned had never failed at anything, and he was determined not to fail in a trade. He went on to express his frustration with his previous mentor. He was fully convinced that he could perform brain surgery, if he just had the right teacher.

At the end of our session, I explained to Ned that I would not be able to help him. He was offended that I could turn down such a naturally gifted student. I wished him well and went on my way. Several years have passed and the last I heard, Ned was still searching.

If you don't accept responsibility for your own actions, then you are powerless to make changes. You can only modify those things that are within your control. When you live in reaction, you have no power. *Figure out what it is that you are doing wrong and fix it rather than blame someone or something.*

"Don't say you don't have enough time. You have exactly the same number of hours per day that were given to Helen Keller, Pasteur, Michelangelo, Mother Teresa, Leonardo da Vinci, Thomas Jefferson, and Albert Einstein."
~ H. Jackson Brown Jr.

61

FORGET EXCUSES, MAKE IT HAPPEN!

You're going to have to *make* time to make this happen. Trading requires a lot of time, energy, dedication, patience, focus, and practice. If you have a full-time job, this is not going to fall in your lap in your free time. You'll have to dedicate hours to learning and studying and growing as a trader. Decide ahead of time how much time, energy, and money you can dedicate, and then create a plan that works within those parameters.

You have to decide on not only a trading style that fits but also a routine that works within your existing responsibilities. Create a plan for how you will learn. Where will the time come from? Take a good look at how you spend your time now and where you can make cuts. How much of your time is spent on activities that are not important, like watching TV or surfing on the net? Your mission statement will help you give up some of these activities when you see what trading can do for your life.

Accept that you don't *have enough time now, but understand that you will have to make the time.*

PIRATE FUN FACT: "Show a leg!" - A phrase used to wake up a sleeping pirate.[2]

"You can't hire someone else to do your pushups for you."
~ Jim Rohn

DO THE WORK TO BUILD CONFIDENCE

You can watch someone swing a golf club all day long, but that is not going to make you a scratch golfer. You need to swing the club yourself to gain the feel of the club, and you must have the strength and muscle control to hit the ball. It's the same in trading. You can watch someone trade, but until you click the button with money from your own account, you are not going to become a trader. What you need is screen time, sitting there watching the market, executing your trades, and learning lessons from your mistakes. When you watch your instructor or mentor trade, you gain more confidence in *his or her* abilities. Watching your mentor draw levels is helpful, but when you see your own levels hit, the ones *you* selected, that's where confidence begins.

You certainly learn a lot by watching a professional, but to actually become successful, you're going to have to *do your own pushups.*

"The road to success is dotted with many tempting parking spaces."
~ Unknown

DON'T GET DISTRACTED

I've met many want-to-be traders who have become experts on how to program an indicator or how to design a spreadsheet to track trades, or who can recite more market babble than CNBC commentators on crack. The problem is that they still haven't learned how to trade. This is a common problem because trading attracts successful people and successful people do not like to fail.

Trading tests our patience, slaps down our confidence, dents our finances, and bruises our ego. After getting beat up in the market, we are tempted to move back into the world where we were successful and things made sense. We want to be able to learn something and have it work consistently. It is difficult to keep trading when it is kicking your butt, but *the road to success is beyond those tempting parking spaces.*

PIRATE FUN FACTS: "Gangway!" - Get out of my way!

"*Of all sad words of tongue or pen, the saddest are these, 'It might have been.'*"
~ *John Greenleaf Whittier, Maud Muller—Pamphlet*

64

DON'T KNOCK YOURSELF OUT OF THE GAME

I wholeheartedly believe that anyone can learn how to trade *if* he or she doesn't run out of money or time. Mary took a year of leave from her job hoping to learn trading as a career. Although she extended it an extra year, she still was not trading. When she went back to her previous position, her trading account was exactly where she started. I was an over-trader; Mary was an under-trader. She was looking for the perfect conditions to enter the market, and they never existed.

Harry came to me at one of our regular monthly meetings. "This will be my last meeting. I've lost $80,000 in four months and I'm going back to work." When I asked him how many contracts he was trading (he was trading futures), he informed me that he had been trading ten. I wanted to tell him that with one contract, he would have had ten times the amount of time to learn, but I decided against it. Mary ran out of time; Harry ran out of money.

One of my favorite stories is at the beginning of *Think and Grow Rich* by Napoleon Hill. He tells the story of Darby who had discovered gold, but soon the fault line ran dry. He continued to drill but eventually gave up and sold his mining equipment to a junkman. The junkman consulted an expert and discovered that Darby had miscalculated the fault line. He had stopped three feet from the gold.

I never forgot this story. When I was learning how to trade, I knew one thing: I would not quit. I simply couldn't live with the thought that if I gave up, I would never know if I had stopped three feet from the gold.

Do what it takes to stay in the game, so you'll never have to wonder *what might have been.*

"It is what we think we know already that often prevents us from learning."
~ Claude Bernard

65

BE TEACHABLE

I've had more than a few students come into class with heads full of "knowledge" about the markets. They've spent more time reading trading books and watching CNBC than a cat covering crap on a marble floor. Unfortunately, it is those students who have the hardest time learning how to trade.

By his third day in class, George was still telling me how he was trading. He didn't directly oppose what was being taught, but he kept telling me, "This is how *I* do it." I knew he was struggling and I tried several times to help him, but it was obvious that he intended to continue with his own ideas. I really wanted to find a way to open his eyes. At the end of day four, I was spending some one-on-one time with students. George began to "teach" me his ways in the market again. I decided to pull out the Dr. Phil card. "So how is that working for you?" He replied, "Well, it's not." It was as if a light bulb was turned on for the first time. George spent the rest of the class like a sponge, soaking up knowledge. Sometimes *it's what we already know that prevents us from learning.*

PIRATE FUN FACT: 'Scallywag' - A villainous or mischievous person.[2]

"Life's hard. It's even harder when you're stupid."
~ John Wayne

LEARN FROM PROFESSIONALS

Many traders spent well over $100,000 donating to the market trying to learn how to trade. Unfortunately, not all of them became traders. Every trader pays for education, but not every trader is educated. You're going to pay for an education one way or the other. For those who don't know what they're doing, they will pay the market. The problem with this process is that many traders cannot afford this education and leave that "school" long before they ever realize any benefit.

You wouldn't walk into a new broker's office and lay a check on his or her desk that includes your entire retirement account without first wanting to know the skill and experience of that individual. The broker would obviously have to provide you with a proven track record of success. Strangely, many people drop that same check on their own desk and begin to trade it with little or no experience or education.

Figuring out that trading didn't fit into my normal path to success required a lot of trial and error. I was using the same process that had served me well in the past: work hard, be persistent, and learn from every book on the subject. When that didn't work, I worked harder, became more persistent, and read more. When that didn't work, I became more and more frustrated. I began to search for people who were making money in the market. I learned that getting your education from professional traders who have already been there and done that is the most cost-effective way to learn how to trade. *Learning how to trade was very hard and I made it even harder in the beginning by being stupid.*

PIRATE FUN FACT: "To go on account" - A pleasant term used by pirates to describe the act of turning pirate. The basic idea was that a pirate was more "free lance" and thus was, more or less, going into business for himself.[2]

"Twenty years from now you will be more disappointed by the things that you didn't do than by the ones you did do. So throw off the bowlines. Sail away from the safe harbor. Catch the trade winds in your sails. Explore. Dream. Discover."
~ Mark Twain

67

INSPIRATION

While learning how to trade, I posted many of these quotes on my monitor. I found them to be an inspiration in the tough times. They were my golden nuggets. I hope they inspire you as well.

"The reason man may become the master of his own destiny is because he has the power to influence his own subconscious mind." ~Napoleon Hill

"Life is a daring adventure or nothing at all." ~ Helen Keller

"If I had to select one quality, one personal characteristic, that I regard as being most highly correlated with success, whatever the field, I would pick the trait of persistence. Determination. The will to endure to the end, to get knocked down seventy times and get up off the floor saying, 'Here comes number seventy-one!'" ~ Richard M. Devos

"In the confrontation between the stream and the rock, the stream always wins - not through strength, but through persistence." ~ Buddha

"It's a weird sensation to be mad and learning at the same time." ~ Jeff Foxworthy

"Courage is going from failure to failure without losing enthusiasm." ~ Winston Churchill*"*

"There are no secrets to success. It is the result of hard work, preparation, and learning from failure." ~ General Colin Powell

"There are no guarantees. There is only the path." ~ Unknown

"We cannot become what we need to be by remaining what we are." ~ Max De Pree

"One day your life will flash before your eyes. Make sure its worth watching."~ Gerard Way

"Life may not be the party we hoped for, but while we're here we should dance." ~ Unknown

"I know of no more encouraging fact than the unquestionable ability of man to elevate his life by conscious endeavor."~ Thoreau

"It is one of the most beautiful compensations of this life that no man can sincerely try to help another without helping himself. "~ Ralph Waldo Emerson

"Effort only fully releases its reward after a person refuses to quit." ~ Napoleon Hill

GLOSSARY

Average Price
A measure of a range of prices paid for a security that is calculated by taking the sum of the prices and dividing them by the number of prices being examined. The average price reduces the range of prices paid into a single value. 63

Bail out
In this context: to exit a trade too early before it has reached the anticipated profit target. 65, 95

Ben Bernanke
Chairman of the Federal Reserve. 53

Big Picture
Can include the economy, overall market direction, conditions around the world or the larger time frames (daily, weekly, monthly). 77

Breakout
A price movement through a level which, historically, a stock has had difficulty rising above or falling below. Traders will buy the underlying asset when the price breaks above a level of resistance and sell when it breaks below support. 63, 75

Breakout tool
Refers to a momentum breakout trading strategy. 75

Bull Market
A financial market or a group of securities in which prices are rising or are expected to rise. The term "bull market" is most often used to refer to the stock market, but can be applied to anything that is traded, such as bonds, currencies and commodities. 61

Buy Stop
An order to buy a security which is entered at a price above the current offering price (in this case to exit a short position). It is triggered

when the market price touches or goes through the buy stop price. 63

Candle
A representation of a price chart that displays the high, low, open, and close for a security over a specified period of time. 33, 87

Chart/Time Chart
One bar will print at the end of each specified time interval. On a 60-minute chart, for example, a bar will print at 9:30, 10:30, 11:30 and so on until the end of the trading session. 51, 77, 87

Contracts
Futures Contract - A contractual agreement, generally made on the trading floor of a futures exchange, to buy or sell a particular commodity or financial instrument at a pre-determined price in the future. Futures contracts detail the quality and quantity of the under-lying asset; they are standardized to facilitate trading on a futures exchange. Some futures contracts may call for physical delivery of the asset, while others are settled in cash. 99, 129

Counter-trend trade
Taking a trade opposite the current momentum direction. 17, 77

Cramer
Host of Mad Money on CNBC. 7, 51

Currency
Currency or Currency Market is a market in which currencies are traded. Also known as the forex market. 21

Curve
Early in the curve of a new trend is closest to the most reccent reversal. Late in the curve of an existing trend is furtherst away from the most recent reversal. 77

Cut a winner short
In this context: to exit a trade too early before it has reached the anticipated profit target. 95

Doubling a position

Doubling a position by Dollar Cost Averaging: Continuing to buy or short a particular investment when it is not going in your favor (rather than exit with a small loss) in hopes of getting back to break even. 93

Dollar Cost Averaging

Doubling a position by Dollar Cost Averaging: Continuing to buy or short a particular investment when it is not going in your favor (rather than exit with a small loss) in hopes of getting back to break even. 93

Dow Jones Industrial Average

A price-weighted average of 30 blue chip stocks. Dow Futures: A futures contract on the Dow index. 27

Downgrade

A negative change in the rating of a security when analysts feel that the future prospects for the security have weakened from the orginal recommendation. 51

Drawdown

The peak-to-trough decline during a specific period of an investment, fund or commodity. A drawdown is usually quoted as the percentage between the peak and the trough. 79, 113

Earnings

The amount of profit that a company produces during a specific period, which is usually defined as a quarter (three calendar months) or a year. 7, 51, 59, 61

Entry

The price at which an investor buys or shorts an investment. The entry point is usually a component of a predetermined trading strategy for minimizing risk and removing the emotion from trading decisions. 55, 79

Execution

Choosing the entry, exit and stop placement, as well as trade management while in the trade. 65

Expanded Range Candle

A candlestick that looks significantly larger than other candles on that chart. An Expanded Range Candle usually indicates strong momentum. 77

Federal Reserve Chairman

The central bank of the United States who regulates the U.S. monetary and financial system. The Federal Reserve System has both private and public components, and was originally designed to serve the interests of both the general public and private bankers. 53

Futures

A financial contract obligating the buyer to purchase an asset (or the seller to sell an asset), such as a physical commodity or a financial instrument, at a predetermined future date and price. Some futures contracts may call for physical delivery of the asset, while others are settled in cash. The futures markets are characterized by the ability to use very high leverage relative to stock markets. Futures can be used either to hedge or to speculate on the price movement of the underlying asset. For example, a producer of corn could use futures to lock in a certain price and reduce risk (hedge). On the other hand, anybody could speculate on the price movement of corn by going long or short using futures. 21

Inside Day

Price has not yet broken yesterday's high or low (it is still trading inside yesterday's range). 75

Institution

A non-bank person or organization that trades securities in large enough share quantities or dollar amounts that they qualify for preferential treatment and lower commissions. Institutional investors face fewer protective regulations because it is assumed that they are more knowledgeable and better able to protect themselves. 9, 61, 63

Intraday

"Within the day". Intraday price movements are particularly important to short-term traders looking to make many trades over the course of a single trading session. The term intraday is occasionally used to describe securities that trade on the markets during regular business hours. 29, 79, 113

Jim Cramer
Host of Mad Money on CNBC. 7, 51

Late entry
Buying or shorting after price has already moved in your favor. The late entry increases the risk and decreases the reward by changing the profit and loss calculations. 83

Let Winners run

Staying in a trade as long as it continues to pay. 75, 77, 89

Lock in
Moving a stop loss to a place on the chart where profits have already been achieved (above the entry point in a long trade or below the entry point in a short trade). 63

Long
The buying of a security such as a stock, commodity or currency, with the expectation that the asset will rise in value. 7, 55

Loss Limit
The maximum loss that is allowed in any one trade or trading session. The limits are set by the trader in an attempt to prevent a large loss. 79, 113

Manage the trade
A pre-planned strategy for moving the stop loss to breakeven or locking in profit only after certain criteria are met (typically after a certain percentage of profit is achieved). 79

Momentum
The rate of acceleration of a security's price or volume. The belief is that price is more likely to keep moving in the same direction. 55, 75

Move stop
Bring the original protective stop closer to current price once the price moves favorably. 63, 65, 79

Noise
Price and volume fluctuations in the market that can confuse one's interpretation of market direction. 87

Pay out
"Refuse to pay out" refers to traders who do not exit a trade that has passed the point where the trade has failed. 93

Point
Point can have several meanings. In this context: a $1 price change in the value of common stock or future. 73, 87

Position
The amount of a security either owned (which constitutes a long position) or borrowed (which constitutes a short position) by an individual or by a dealer. In other words, it's a trade an investor currently holds open. 7, 47

Position traders
A style of trading that attempts to capture larger gains in a stock over a longer period of time than intraday or swing trading. 79, 113

Range Bound or Choppy
Stocks trading in channels, finding major support and resistance levels. This offers an opportunity for a trader to buy stocks at the lower level of support (bottom of the channel) and sell them near resistance (top of the channel). When the range is too small, it is very difficult to make a profit. 75, 77

Recovery mode
The feeling that one needs to get their money back from the market after a loss. 49, 85, 113

Retrace
A pullback in price, a counter-trend move. 63

Revenge Trading
Revenge trading means continuing to trade after a loss because the markets took your money and you have to get it back. 47, 113

Reversal
A change in market direction. 77

Screen time
Watching the market, executing trades, and learning lessons from mistakes. 125

Sector
1. An area of the economy in which businesses share the same or a related product or service. 2. An industry or market sharing common characteristics. 59

Share
A measure used in the financial world to illustrate the quantity for one share of a company's stock. A type of security that signifies ownership in a corporation and represents a claim on part of the corporation's assets and earnings. 99, 101

Short/Sell Short
The selling of a security that the seller does not own, or any sale that is completed by the delivery of a security borrowed by the seller. Short sellers assume that they will be able to buy the stock at a lower amount than the price at which they sold short. 5, 53, 57, 63, 89

Stock
A type of security that signifies ownership in a corporation and represents a claim on part of the corporation's assets and earnings. Also known as "shares" or "equity". 59

Stop or Stop Loss Order
An order placed with a broker to sell a security when it reaches a certain price. A stop-loss order is designed to limit an investor's loss on a security position. 5, 17, 23, 65, 79, 85

Stopped out
The execution of a stop-loss order. 35, 81, 85

Strategy
A well-defined systematic process of buying and selling stocks or other products. 13, 41, 69

Strong stock
   A stock that is moving up with good strong momentum. 55

Supply-and-Demand
   An area on the chart where there were more buyers than sellers (demand) or more sellers than buyers (supply). 23, 25, 75, 97

Swing
   A style of trading that attempts to capture gains in a stock within one to four days. 79, 113

Technical Indicator
   Any class of metrics whose value is derived from generic price activity in a stock or asset. Technical indicators look to predict the future price levels, or simply the general price direction, of a security by looking at past patterns. 69

Tick
   The minimum upward or downward movement in the price of a security. The term "tick" also refers to the change in the price of a security from trade to trade. 75, 81

Tick Chart
   Tick charts show a certain number of transactions per bar. In a 144-tick chart, for example, one bar will print after every 144 transactions (trades that occur). These transactions include small orders as well as large, block orders.

Time Frame
   A variety of charts, such as monthly, weekly, daily or 60 minute. 77, 87

Top
   A level which a stock has had difficulty rising above in the past. 77

Trading Capital
   The amount of money allotted to buying and selling various securities. 71

Trading Plan

A written plan detailing the systematic method for trading. It might include screening and evaluating stocks, a specific setup, determining the amount of risk , formulating objectives, trade managment,trading rules, and the type of trading system to be used. 15

Trap

A false signal that the trend of a stock or index has reversed when it has not. 61

Trend

The general direction of a market or of the price of an asset. Trends can vary in length from short, to intermediate, to long term. A trend trader might invest based on the ups and downs of the market, not on the strengths of the firms whose stock he traded. 23, 75, 77

Upgrade

A positive change in the rating of a security. An upgrade is usually triggered by a steady improvement in the fundamentals and financials of the entity that has issued the security. 7

Wicks

Wicks are also known as shadows or tails. A small line found on a candle in a candlestick chart that is used to indicate where the price of a stock has fluctuated relative to the opening and closing prices. The wicks or shadows illustrate the highest and lowest prices at which a security has traded over a specific time period. 77

Win Loss Ratio

A ratio of the total number of winning trades to the number of losing trades. It does not take into account how much was won or lost simply if they were winners or losers. 89, 91

FOOTNOTES

1. http:// www.piratesinfo.com
2. http:// www.pirateglossary.com
3. http:// www.talklikeapirate.com
4. http://www.tide-mark.com
5. http://www.piratetreasurenow.com
6. http://www.sayingsplus.com

Made in the USA
Lexington, KY
08 June 2019